# REASON AND REVELATION

# IN THE MIDDLE AGES

*by* ETIENNE GILSON

Also published by Charles Scribner's Sons

THE SPIRIT OF MEDIAEVAL PHILOSOPHY
THE UNITY OF PHILOSOPHICAL EXPERIENCE

# REASON AND REVELATION
# IN THE MIDDLE AGES

By

Etienne Gilson

———

CHARLES SCRIBNER'S SONS · NEW YORK

COPYRIGHT 1938 CHARLES SCRIBNER'S SONS;
RENEWAL COPYRIGHT © 1966 ETIENNE GILSON

5 7 9 11 13 15 17 19 Y/P 20 18 16 14 12 10 8 6 4

Printed in the United States of America

ISBN 0-684-15026-3

To my friend

ALBERT G. A. BALZ

*Corcoran Professor of Philosophy
in the University of
Virginia*

# Foreword

*It is a pleasant duty, for visiting lecturers, to begin by expressing their gratitude to their hosts. In no case would I have forgotten to do it. But my indebtedness to the University of Virginia has far deeper roots than this occasion, the Richard Lectures for 1937. It was my privilege, eleven years ago, to begin my first visit to the United States by spending half a day in New York and nearly two months in Charlottesville. I say it was a privilege, because the memory of the days I have spent in this University has ever since remained with me, as a safeguard against the temptation, fatal to foreigners, to explore America from the top of the Empire State Building. To the friends and colleagues who then invited me, but no less to the students of the Summer School of 1926, who kindly helped me through a difficult task, I beg to renew today the expression of my lasting gratitude.*

ETIENNE GILSON.

# Contents

# CHAPTER
# ONE

# I

---

# The Primacy of Faith

THE SUBJECT of these chapters not only recommends itself to us by its intrinsic merits, but it also provides an unusually favorable occasion to exercise that essential function of university teaching, the criticism of commonly received opinions. This criticism, which is obviously relevant in a positive science, is no less relevant in history. Now it is not unusual, in textbooks of general history, to distinguish three main periods in the development of Western thought. There first comes the age of Greek philosophy, the so-called "Greek miracle," a sort of Golden Age of human thought, that witnessed the quiet and undisturbed triumph of pure rational knowledge. Next come the Middle Ages, also called the Dark Ages, because from the rise of

Christianity to the dawn of the Renaissance, the
normal use of natural reason was obscured by blind
faith in the absolute truth of Christian Revelation.
Philosophy then became a mere tool at the hands of
unscrupulous theologians until at last, around the
end of the fifteenth century, the joint effort of the
humanists, of the scientists and of the religious reformers gave rise to the new era of purely positive
and rational speculation in which we still find ourselves engaged.

What an historian of Greek philosophy can
think of so simplified a view of his own field of
studies, I am not prepared to say. Nor am I planning to discuss such views with regard to modern
philosophy, but it is my intention, in these chapters, to test their truth value in so far as the Middle Ages are concerned. And I beg to make this
quite clear, from the very beginning, that I am not
at all planning to defend the Middle Ages against
what is most certainly an unfair interpretation.
I shall not even attempt to define and to maintain
a new one. Of the Middle Ages as a whole, I have
indeed no interpretation. But we can hope to
achieve, if not a description of those seven cen-

turies of abstract speculation, at least a sketch of
the main spiritual families which were responsible
for the copious philosophical and theological lit-
erature of the Middle Ages. I am too well aware
of the fact that even so modest a result cannot be
achieved without some violence done to the irre-
ducible originality of the various medieval thinkers. We shall have sometimes to group together
some men who would have taken no pleasure in
finding themselves in the same class. It may nevertheless be hoped that our classification will prove
as natural as classifications of human types can
possibly be. At any rate, it should not be considered a waste of time to substitute for the
usually received one a less conventional conven-
tion.

The first of those spiritual families, and the
only one we will now attempt to characterize, was
made up of those theologians according to whom
Revelation had been given to men as a substitute
for all other knowledge, including science, ethics
and metaphysics. Ever since the very origin of
Christianity up to our own days, there have always been such extremists in theology. Reduced

to its essentials, their position is very simple; since God has spoken to us, it is no longer necessary for us to think. The only thing that matters for every one of us is to achieve his own salvation; now all that we need to know in order to achieve it is there, written down in the Holy Scriptures; let us therefore read the divine law, meditate upon it, live according to its precepts, and we shall stand in need of nothing else, not even of philosophy. I should rather say: particularly *not* of philosophy. In point of fact, we shall do infinitely better without philosophical knowledge than with it. Consider even the greatest among the Greek philosophers, including those whose teaching more or less resembled that of Christian Revelation, and you will find it everywhere at variance with the contents of Christian Revelation. Plato believed in an eternal transmigration of souls from their former bodies to other human, or even animal bodies. Aristotle denied Divine Providence and did not even believe in the personal immortality of the soul. The Stoics and the Epicureans were materialists. Even if we assume that what they claimed to know about God

were true, what are we going to say about that
which God Himself has revealed to us, and which
they certainly did not know? Can man be saved
unless he knows the fact of original sin, the Incarnation of Christ, the redemption of man
through His death on the cross, and grace, and
the Church with its sacraments? If such have been
the errors and the shortcomings of the greatest
among philosophical geniuses, their very blindness
in matters of vital importance, there is no reason
why true Christians should pay the slightest attention to what philosophers may have said on
those questions. As Saint Paul himself once said:
"Professing themselves to be wise, they become
fools." (Rom. 1:22.) And again: "For seeing
that in the wisdom of God the world by wisdom
knew not God, it pleased God, by the foolishness
of our preaching, to save them that believe. . . .
the foolishness of God is wiser than men." (I Cor.
1:21, 25.) In short, since he who merely believes
in the word of God knows more than the greatest philosophers have ever known concerning the
only matters of vital importance, we should feel
justified in saying that the simplest among Chris-

tians has a philosophy of his own, which is the only true philosophy, and whose name is: Revelation.*[1]

This absolute conviction in the self-sufficiency of Christian Revelation has always found decided supporters. We find it represented in all the significant periods of the history of Christian thought; its representatives are always there, but it becomes vocal chiefly during such times when philosophy is threatening to invade the field of Revelation. As early as the second century, when gnosticism became a real danger, Tertullian found forceful formulas to stress what he held to be an irreconcilable antagonism between Christianity and philosophy. The seventh chapter of his treatise *On prescription against heretics* is but a violent attack against what the Lord Himself called the "foolishness" of philosophy: "For philosophy it is which is the material of the world's wisdom, the rash interpreter of the nature and dispensation of God. Indeed heresies are themselves instigated by philosophy. The same subject matter is discussed over and over again by the heretics

*The footnotes, being almost entirely of a bibliographical nature, have been placed at the back of the book.

and the philosophers; the same arguments are involved. Whence comes evil? Why is it permitted?
What is the origin of man? And in what way does
he come? Besides the question which Valentius
has very lately proposed—Whence comes God?
Which he settles with the answer: From *enthymesis* and *ectroma*. Unhappy Aristotle! who invented for these men dialectics, the art of building up and pulling down, an art so far-fetched
in its conjectures, so harsh in its arguments, so
productive of contentions—embarrassing even to
itself, retracting everything, and really treating
of nothing!" Has not Saint Paul already warned
us from such dangerous speculations, when he
wrote to the Colossians, saying: "Beware lest any
man cheat you by philosophy, and vain deceit;
according to the tradition of men . . . and not
according to Christ." (Col. 2:8.) Until at last,
giving rein to his eloquent indignation, Tertullian exclaims: "What indeed has Athens to do
with Jerusalem? What concord is there between
the Academy and the Church? what between heretics and Christians? Our instruction comes from
the porch of Solomon (Acts 3:5) who had him-

self taught that the Lord should be sought in simplicity of heart. (Wisd. 1:1.) Away with all attempts to produce a mottled Christianity of Stoic, Platonic and dialectic composition! We want no curious disputation after possessing Christ Jesus, no inquisition after enjoying the Gospel! With our faith, we desire no further belief. For this is our palmary faith, that there is nothing which we ought to believe besides."[2]

I have quoted Tertullian at some length, because of the very perfection with which he exemplifies that typical attitude. All its essential features are already there, and I do not think we could find a single one of these sentences that was not quoted again and again from the second century until the end of the Middle Ages, or even later. Let us call this family the Tertullian family, and I am sure you will never fail to identify its members when you meet them. In spite of their personal differences, the species itself is so easily recognizable! Emphasis laid upon three or four texts of Saint Paul, always the same, and exclusion of all his other statements about our natural knowledge of God, and the existence, nay, the

binding force of a natural moral law; unquali-
fied condemnation of Greek philosophy, as though
no Greek philosopher had ever said anything true
concerning the nature of God, of man and of our
destiny; bitter hatred, and vicious attacks especially directed against Dialectics, as if it were
possible even to condemn Dialectics without making use of it; the tracing back of heresies against
religious dogmas to the pernicious influence of
philosophical speculation upon theological knowledge; last, not the least, the crude statement of
an absolute opposition between religious faith in
the word of God and the use of natural reason in
matters pertaining to Revelation; all those features, whose interrelation is obvious, help in defining the members of the Tertullian family and
in perceiving what confers upon the group at
least a loose unity of its own.

To limit ourselves to a small number of typical
cases, let us recall the Greek writer Tatian, whose
*Address to the Greeks* is but the violent protest
of a Christian barbarian against the pride which
the pagan Greeks were taking in their so-called
civilized institutions. "What noble thing have you

produced by your pursuit of philosophy?" Tatian
asks. And after a long series of attacks against
Plato and Aristotle, the Stoics and the Epicureans, we find him in full agreement with the conclusion of Tertullian, whom he had certainly not
read: "Obeying the commands of God, and following the law of the Father of immortality, we
reject everything which rests upon human opinion."[3] If we pass from the second to the twelfth
century, in a time when the magnificent development of Logic could not but worry men of the
Tertullian family, we find interesting specimens
of this fierce theological species. The great Saint
Bernard himself exhibited some of their traits.
He probably had Peter Abelard in mind while he
was writing his third *Sermon for the Feast of
Pentecost*. At any rate, Bernard had obviously
no use for those men who "called themselves philosophers," but, in his own opinion, "should rather
be called the slaves of curiosity and pride." He
did not want his brethren to belong to this school,
but rather to the school of that supreme teacher
to whom the feast of Pentecost is dedicated: the
Holy Ghost. Because they had indeed attended

His divine school, each of them could say with the Psalmist (Ps. 119:99) : *I have understood more than all my teachers.* And carried away by his admirable eloquence, Bernard suddenly exclaimed: "Wherefore, O my brother, dost thou make such a boast? Is it because . . . thou has understood or hast endeavored to understand the reasonings of Plato and the subtleties of Aristotle? God forbid! thou answerest. It is because I have sought Thy commandments, O Lord."[4] Saint Peter Damiani, with his much more vicious attacks on Dialectics, Grammar, and generally speaking all that which involved the slightest reliance upon the power of natural reason, would be a still more complete, though much less lovable instance of the same tendency.[5] In the thirteenth and four-teenth centuries, the passionate and, at times, sav-age controversy that raged, within the Franciscan Order, between its extremists—the so-called Spir-ituals, and the partisans of a well-conducted study of philosophy—had no other cause than the radi-cal theologism of those Spirituals. The Franciscan poet Jacopone da Todo was a Spiritual, and he merely voiced their common feeling when he wrote,

in one of his most famous poems: "Paris has de-
stroyed Assise," and again:

> Plato and Socrates may contend
> And all the breath in their bodies spend,
> Arguing without an end—
> What's it all to me?
> Only a pure and simple mind
> Straight to heaven its way doth find;
> Greets the King—while far behind
> Lags the world's philosophy.[6]

The partisans of exclusive otherworldliness in
the order of knowledge have been present wherever and whenever churchmen were interested in
scientific and philosophical studies to the point of
becoming actively engaged in the task of fostering
their progress. The devil who visited Albertus
Magnus in his cell, while the Saint was busy in
solving some scientific problem, must have been a
particularly clever unclean spirit, since he managed
to appear in the garb of a Dominican Friar. And
what was his message to the Saint? Simply that
he was spending his time in occupations foreign to
his profession, and should devote less time to sci-

ence, but more to theology. Then, the old Chronicle goes on to say: "Albert, interiorly warned by the Divine Spirit of the impostor's design, contented himself with making the sign of the cross, and the phantom disappeared."⁷ So much theological zeal in a devil was bound to look suspicious.

Had the Middle Ages produced men of this type only, the period would fully deserve the title of Dark Ages which it is commonly given. It would deserve the name not only from the point of view of science and of philosophy, but from that of theology as well. Fortunately, the history of Christian thought attests the existence of another spiritual family, much more enlightened than the first one, and whose untiring efforts to blend religious faith with rational speculations have achieved really important results. No less than those of the first group, the members of the second could find in the Bible texts to justify their own attitude. Not only had Saint Paul clearly stated that even pagans should be able to achieve a natural knowledge of the existence of God, "his eternal power also and divinity, so that they are

inexcusable" (Rom. 1:20), but, in the first chapter of his Gospel, Saint John also had said that
the Word of God "was the true light, which en-
lighteneth every man that cometh into this
world." (John 1:9.) No wonder then that the
greatest among the Greek Fathers of the Church
—Justin Martyr, Clement of Alexandria, and
Origen—built up theological doctrines in which the
fundamental agreement of natural and revealed
knowledge was everywhere either stated or pre-
supposed. Yet, by far the most perfect represen-
tative of this group was, and is very likely to remain, a Latin Father—Saint Augustine. For the
sake of brevity, and using the name as a mere
practical label, let us call the representatives of
this second tendency the Augustinian family.
What were its essential characteristics?

We all remember the chapters of his *Confes-
sions*, where Augustine relates how, after vainly
trying to reach truth, and eventually faith, by
means of reason alone, he had at last discovered
that all the rational truth about God that had
been taught by the philosophers could be grasped
at once, pure of all errors, and enriched with many

a more than philosophical truth by the simple act
of faith of the most illiterate among the faithful.
From that time on, Augustine was never to forget
that the safest way to reach truth is not the one
that starts from reason and then goes on from rational certitude to faith, but, on the contrary, the
way whose starting point is faith and then goes on
from Revelation to reason.

By reaching that unexpected conclusion, Augustine was opening a new era in the history of
western thought. No Greek philosopher could
have ever dreamt of making religious faith in some
revealed truth the obligatory starting point of rational knowledge. In point of fact, Socrates,
Plato, Aristotle, the Stoics and even the Epicureans, had always been busy in refining and rationally reinterpreting the crude myths of Greek
paganism. By far the highest type of religious
thought among the Ancients was that of their philosophers. With Saint Augustine, on the contrary,
a new age was beginning, in which by far the
highest type of philosophical thinking would be
that of the theologians. True enough, even the
faith of an Augustinian presupposes a certain ex-

ercise of natural reason. We cannot believe something, be it the word of God Himself, unless we find some sense in the formulas which we believe. And it can hardly be expected that we will believe in God's Revelation, unless we be given good reasons to think that such a Revelation has indeed taken place. As modern theologians would say, there are motives of credibility. Yet, when all is said, the most forceful reasons to believe that God has spoken cannot take us further than that belief itself. Now to believe that God has spoken, and that what God has said is true, is something essentially different from a rational comprehension of the truth which we hold by faith. We *believe* that it is true, but no Christian can hope to *know*, at least in this life, the truth which he believes. Yet, among those truths which he believes, the Christian finds the divine promise later to contemplate the God of his faith, and in that contemplation, to find eternal beatitude; hence, already in this life, his passionate effort to investigate the mysteries of Revelation by the natural light of reason. The result of such an effort is precisely what Augustine used to call *intellectus; understanding*, that is to say, some rational insight into the contents of Revelation, human reason groping its way towards the full light of the beatific vision.

Such is the ultimate meaning of Augustine's famous formula: "Understanding is the reward of faith. Therefore seek not to understand that thou mayest believe, but believe that thou mayest understand."[8] And again, in a longer but much more complete statement: "If to believe were not one thing and to understand another, and unless we had first to believe the great and divine thing which we desire to understand, the Prophet would have spoken idly when he said: 'Unless you believe, you shall not understand.' (Is. 7:9; secund. 70.) Our Lord Himself, too, by His words and deeds exhorted those whom He called to salvation, that they first believe. But afterwards, when He was talking of the gift which He would give to believers, He did not say, 'This is eternal life that you may *believe*,' but 'This is eternal life: that they may *know* Thee, the only true God, and Jesus Christ Whom Thou hast sent.' (John 17:13.) Furthermore, He said to those who were already believers, 'Seek and you shall find.' (Matt.

7:7.) For what is believed unknown cannot be called found, nor is any one capable of finding God, unless he first believe that he will eventually find Him. . . . That which we seek on His exhortation, we shall find by His showing it to us, so far as it is possible to such as us to find this in this life . . . and we must surely believe that after this life this will be perceived and attained more clearly and more perfectly."⁹

It thus appears from Augustine's explicit statement, first that we are invited by Revelation itself to believe, that unless we believe we shall not understand; next that far from inviting us to do away with reason, the Gospel itself has promised to all those who seek truth in the revealed word the reward of understanding. Whence it follows that instead of entailing its ultimate rejection the doctrine of Saint Augustine was achieving a transfiguration of the Greek ideal of philosophical wisdom. What the greatest among the Pagans, such as Plato and Plotinus, had always been hoping for, was now at hand. For the Greek philosophers had passionately loved wisdom, but grasp it they could not; and there it now was, offered by God Himself to all men as a means of salvation by faith, and, to the philosophers, as an unerring guide towards rational understanding.

From the fourth century after Christ till our own days, there have always been men to uphold, or to revive, the Augustinian ideal of Christian Wisdom. All the members of the Augustinian family resemble one another by their common acceptance of the fundamental principle: unless you believe, you shall not understand. Moreover, being Christians, all of them agree that the only conceivable faith is faith in Christian Revelation. Yet, despite their unmistakable family air, the members of that remarkably united family have always been conspicuous by their personal originality. You cannot fail to know an Augustinian when you meet one in history, but it is not an easy thing to guess what he is going to say. The reason for it is, that while all the members of the family hold the same faith, in whatever places and times they happen to live, not all of them use their understanding in the same way. The faith upheld by Augustine in the fourth century was substantially the same one as that of Saint

Anselm in the eleventh century, of Saint Bonaventura in the thirteenth, of Malebranche in the
seventeenth, and of Gioberti in the nineteenth, but
while their common set of beliefs exhibits this remarkable stability, the received views on the proper
use of human reason were constantly changing
around them. In short, all the Augustinians agree
that unless we believe, we shall not understand;
and all of them agree as to what we should believe,
but they do not always agree as to what it is to
understand.

Hence the remarkable aptness of the Augustinian family to stand the test of time. The most
drastic intellectual revolutions merely provide Augustinians with a new occasion to manifest their
permanent vitality. To Saint Augustine himself,
the perfect type of rational knowledge was the
philosophy of Plato, as revised and brought up to
date by Plotinus. Consequently, given his own idea
of what rational knowledge is, the whole philosophical activity of Saint Augustine had to be a
rational interpretation of the Christian Revelation, in terms of platonic philosophy. As Saint
Thomas Aquinas was later going to say: Augustine

has followed in the wake of the Platonists as far as
he could possibly go with them.[10] The most ex-
acting historical research can but confirm Thomas'
statement. The Augustinian conceptions of man,
of the relations of soul and body, of sense knowledge and of intellectual knowledge, are obviously
Christian reinterpretations of the corresponding
notions in both Plato and Plotinus. By attempting
such reinterpretations from a Christian point of
view, Augustine was condemned to being original.
In all his works, the platonic frame is, so to speak,
bursting under the internal pressure of its Christian contents. That was unavoidable in most cases,
but quite particularly when Augustine had to turn
the plotinian Logos into the Word of Saint John,
or to transmute the platonic doctrine of reminis-
cence into a Christian doctrine of the divine illumination.[11] Yet, when all is said, it still must be maintained that the net result of Augustine's philosophical speculation was to achieve a platonic
understanding of the Christian Revelation.

Let us now consider another thinker of the same
type, Saint Anselm of Canterbury. As he himself
repeatedly said, his only ambition was to restate

what his master Augustine had already stated.
And that is exactly what he did.[12] Moreover, Anselm was so fully convinced of the validity of
Augustine's method that its most perfect definitions are to be looked for in the writings of Anselm
rather than in those of Augustine. Anselm, not
Augustine, is responsible for the famous formula:
*credo ut intelligam:* "I do not endeavor, O Lord,
to penetrate thy sublimity for in no wise do I com-
pare my understanding with that; but I long to
understand in some degree thy truth, which my
heart believes and loves. For I do not seek to understand that I may believe, but I believe in order to
understand. For this also I believe, that unless I
believed, I should not understand."[13] But Anselm
wrote his treatises during the last years of the
eleventh century; he had not gone through the
ordeal of Augustine's conversion and was not in-
debted to Plato, nor to Plotinus, for his discovery
of what intellectual knowledge actually is. To him,
as to all his contemporaries, rational knowledge was
logical knowledge. In his mind, and in the mind of
his disciples, a rational demonstration was a dialectical demonstration made up of faultlessly

knitted syllogisms. In short, in Anselm's own times, the standard science was Logic. Under such circumstances, the same endeavor, to achieve a rational understanding of Christian faith, was bound to result in a new translation of Christian beliefs into terms of logical demonstration.

Why, for instance, did Anselm ever think of what we now call his "ontological proof" of the existence of God? Because a purely logical demonstration of the existence of God had to be wholly *a priori*, that is, deduced from the sole concept of God, without resorting to empirical knowledge. Whatever its ultimate metaphysical implications may be, the so-called ontological argument is an essentially dialectical deduction of the existence of God, whose internal necessity is that of the principle of contradiction. God is that than which nothing greater can be conceived; if it can be shown that it is contradictory to think of the greatest conceivable being as non-existing, God's existence will have been fully demonstrated. And there will be no use in arguing, with Gaunilo and Saint Thomas, that what such a proof verifies is merely this, that it is impossible for us to think of

God as not existing; for indeed a logician does not need more than that to get full rational satisfaction. As a Christian, Anselm believes there is a God; as a logician, he concludes that the notion of a non-existing God is a self-contradictory notion; since he can neither believe that there is no God, nor conceive it, there follows that God exists. By means of Logic alone, Anselm has achieved a rational understanding of Christian faith—the same faith as that of Augustine, but a different understanding.

Once a Christian thinker gets to this point, nothing could prevent him from applying the same method to each of the Christian dogmas. And indeed Anselm of Canterbury, as well as his immediate disciples, remain famous in the history of theology for their recklessness in giving rational demonstrations of all revealed truths. To limit ourselves to Anselm himself, we find him proving, by conclusive dialectical arguments, not only the Trinity of the Divine Persons, as he did in both his *Monologium* and his *Proslogium*, but even the very Incarnation of Christ, including all its essential modalities, as he did in his *Cur Deus homo.*

As he himself says in his Preface, the first part of
that treatise, "leaving Christ out of view, as if
nothing had ever been known of Him, proves, by
necessary reasons, the impossibility that any man
should be saved without Him. Again, in the second
book, likewise as if nothing were known of Christ, it
is moreover shown as no less patent rational truth,
that human nature was ordained for that purpose,
*viz.* that some time the whole man should enjoy a
happy immortality, both in body and in soul; and
that it was necessary that this design for which
man was made should be fulfilled; but that it could
not be fulfilled unless God became man, so that all
things which we hold with regard to Christ had
necessarily to take place."[14] This bold ambition to
procure necessary reasons for the revealed dogmas
had never entered the mind of Saint Augustine;
but it was bound to follow from a merely dialectical
treatment of Christian faith. The original character of the doctrine of Saint Anselm, and the
peculiar aspect which it still offers to the investi-
gating historian, have no other source and can be
accounted for in no other way.

Let us now jump over the twelfth century and

the Augustinian landscape will once more appear
to us as both constant in its general outline, and
different in its population. The same Christian
Revelation is still there, and there still are men
whose ambition it is to understand it. For what is
wisdom indeed, if not the rational understanding
of faith? But again, what is it to understand? To
such a man as Roger Bacon, who was writing in
the second half of the thirteenth century, there
was no doubt that Logic is a necessary instrument
for anyone who wishes to acquire knowledge; but
at the same time, Bacon was of the opinion that his
contemporaries were overrating its value. His own
contribution to the epistemology of the Middle
Ages was to be a stronger emphasis upon two
rational methods much too neglected in the thirteenth-century universities: mathematical demonstration and experimental investigation. Such had
been his main discovery and it is enough to open
any one of his later works in order to find it there,
under the form of either its statement or some one
of its many applications.

Mathematics, Bacon says, is superior to all the
other sciences, at least in this, that "in mathematics

we are able to arrive at the full truth without error, and at a certainty of all points involved without doubt. . . . But in other sciences, the assistance of mathematics being excluded, there are so many doubts, so many opinions on the part of man, that these sciences cannot be unfolded . . . ; for in these sciences there are from nature no processes of drawing figures and of reckonings, by which all things must be proved true. And therefore in mathematics alone is there certainty without doubt."[15] If a man thus minded happens to be, at the same time, not only a Christian, and a priest, and a Grey Friar, but a member of the Augustinian family, we can be sure that he will not be slow in using mathematics as a means towards the highest of his intellectual ends: achieving some understanding of Christian Revelation. Hence, in the *Opus majus* of Roger Bacon, his curious attempts at representing and expressing, by means of numbers and of geometrical figures, the mysteries of grace and predestination, the relationship between the unity of God and the Trinity of the Divine Persons, the necessarily low proportion of the just ones as compared with the number of the sinners and many other religious teachings of un-equal importance.[16] But experimental science is still much more important than mathematics in the eyes of Roger Bacon; for it is true that mathe-matical demonstrations are binding, but they can do no more than convince us of the truth, they do not show it. Experiments make us see it, and such is the reason why even mathematics must sometimes resort to experimental demonstrations. Why not then add internal experiment to the external one? Mysticism will thus become an experimental knowl-edge of the revealed truth, nay, of all truth what-soever, for it is a clear thing that he who has had diligent training in the use of the spiritual senses will be able "to assure himself and others not only in regard to things spiritual, but also in regard to all human sciences." To Bacon all knowledge is but a particular case of a universal revelation.[17]

Bacon was not to be the last known variety of the Augustinian species. Ramon Lull, who died in 1315, had also discovered a new way of proving truth, which he described at great length in his *Ars magna*, that is, his *Art of proving truth*. By combining together various symbols inscribed on concentric circles, Lull hoped to deduce the whole body of human knowledge in an almost mechanical way.[18] The only trouble with his complicated machine is that his disciples have never been able to agree as to the correct way of using it. But Lull himself could use it, and he applied its principles in another of his works, the *Book of Demonstrations*, where we still can find his demonstrations of the most hidden mysteries, including the Incarnation and the Trinity. To extract from his symbolic logic necessary and incontrovertible arguments in favor of the revealed truth, was his own way to achieve its understanding. True enough the only knowledge that is required from man for his salvation is faith; but as Understanding says in Lull's *Dialogue between Faith and Understanding:* "Those who *can* understand, *should* understand."[19] A perfect motto indeed for the whole Augustinian and Anselm tradition.

Even the most obstinate writer has to stop somewhere; let us therefore take leave of those medieval theologians, but not without stressing the grave difficulties that arise from a thus understood Christian Wisdom. These difficulties do not flow from any internal inconsistency to be found in its notion, but rather from the conditions required for its exercise. The combination of religious holiness with speculative genius always remains an open possibility, and every time it materializes, Christian Wisdom is at hand. To such men as Saint Anselm and Saint Augustine, religious faith is there, objectively defined in its contents by Revelation, as a reality wholly independent from their own personal preferences. In Malebranche's striking formula, religious dogmas are their "experiments" in matters of philosophy. Just as scientists accept observable facts as the very stuff which they have to understand, those religious geniuses accept the data of Revelation as the given facts which they have to understand. Yet, possible as it is, the happy combination of so widely different gifts must needs be rare. What more usually happens is, that instead of using science and philosophy to gain some insight into the rational meaning of Revelation, second-rate thinkers will use Revelation as a substitute for rational knowledge, not without causing serious damage to both Revelation and Reason. The net result of such mistakes always is, first, to render a truly natural knowledge impossible, and next to substitute for faith in the word of God a more or less rational assent to the conclusions of pseudo-demonstrations. Thus confronted with a wisdom of Christians, elaborated by Christians and for the exclusive benefit of Christians, unbelievers find themselves in a rather awkward position. They do not believe, hence they have nothing to understand. The only way out of such a situation is for them to pit against theology a purely philosophical wisdom, exclusively based upon the principles of natural reason and independent of religious revelation. By whom that ideal of a purely philosophical wisdom was upheld in the Middle Ages is the problem which the next chapter will take into consideration.

# CHAPTER
## TWO

# II

---

# The Primacy of Reason

THE ORIGINS of modern rationalism are commonly traced back to the intellectual revolution which took place early in Italy, when such men as Galileo made their first scientific discoveries. And I am very far from saying that there is nothing true in that assertion. Some aspects at least of modern rationalism would not be what they are, and they are among the most significant ones, without the scientific Renaissance of the sixteenth century. The fact remains, however, that there has been another rationalism, much older than that of the Renaissance, and wholly unrelated to any scientific discovery. It was a purely philosophical rationalism, born in Spain, in the mind of an Arabian philosopher, as a conscious reaction against the theologism of the Arabian divines. The author of that reaction was Ibn Rochd, better

37

known to us under the latinized form of his name:
Averroës. When Averroës died, in 1198, he be-
queathed to his successors the ideal of a purely
rational philosophy, an ideal whose influence was
to be such that, by it, the evolution even of Christian philosophy was to be deeply modified.

The rise of what we now call Averroism would
remain a mystery if we did not know that, ever
since the ninth century, many theological dialec-
ticians had been working at establishing some
conciliation between philosophical knowledge and
Islamic faith. Those men had found themselves in
just the same situation as the Fathers of the
Church and the first scholastic theologians. On the
one hand, they had at their disposal translations
of the writings of Aristotle, plus a compilation
known as *The Theology of Aristotle*, though it
was but a collection of texts chiefly borrowed from
the *Enneads* of Plotinus. On the other hand, they
had their own revealed book, the Koran, and the
problem for them was how to think as Aristotle if
we believe as Mohammed.

The greatest among the predecessors of Averroës, Ibn Sina (Avicenna), had succeeded in solv-

ing that difficult problem by building up a philosophy whose crowning part was a natural theology,
thus leaving a door open to the supernatural light
of Revelation. What Avicenna really thought of
the rational value of religious beliefs is not quite
clear. If, as there are good reasons to believe, he
did not make much of them, he at least was clever
enough never to entangle himself in serious theological difficulties. And yet, the man who was, and
remains even in our own days, the greatest theologian in Islam, Gazali, was not slow in noticing a
serious divergence between the authentic teachings
of the Koran and the conclusions of Avicenna.
After summing up the main theses of Avicenna,
he refuted them in his *Destruction of the Philoso-*
*phers*, and endeavored to prove, by rational demonstrations, the fundamental articles of the Moslem
creed.

It is typical of Averroës that he took up the
challenge of Gazali, and, against his theological
*Destruction of the Philosophers*, wrote a *Destruc-*
*tion of the Destruction*. To Averroës, the absolute
truth was not to be found in any sort of Revelation, but in the writings of Aristotle, which he never

tired of commenting on and annotating. When Aristotle had said something, reason itself had spoken, and there was nothing more to say about it. What then should we do, in those many cases where the conclusions of Aristotle seem to contradict the religious beliefs of the community? The bitter hatred of the Moslem divines, and their persecution against him, would not allow Averroës to ignore the question. He dealt with it in his treatise: *The Agreement of Religion and Philosophy,* a landmark in the history of western civilization.

The very title of this treatise is a safe indication that Averroës had no desire to hurt the feelings of the theologians. It must even be said that Averroës was really hoping to convince the theologians, that some sort of agreement between religious faith and philosophical reason was not an absolute impossibility. He certainly was of the opinion that no conflicts should arise between a faith which keeps its own place and a philosophy which is intelligent enough to realize the specific function of religion. The only problem is, what is that place and what is that function?

Averroës opens his discussion of the problem by

observing, that far from condemning the use of philosophical speculation, Revelation itself positively prescribes it. It is an imperative injunction of the religious law, that men should study the nature of things, that they may raise their minds to the knowledge of their common maker. But is not that also the proper business of philosophy? And if it is, does not Revelation itself make it a duty for us to philosophize? Now, no man can be asked to create philosophy out of nothing. Metaphysics is a very old science, which has already been cultivated for several centuries, especially by the Greeks. Consequently, Revelation cannot' prescribe the study of philosophy without enjoining at the same time the study of Greek philosophy. Nor is that all. The Divine Law explicitly makes obligatory the observation and interpretation of nature by reason, so that we may infer God from His creation. But an inference is a definite mode of reasoning, and nobody can use it properly unless he knows first what are the various kinds of dialectical arguments and in what way the necessary conclusions of reason differ from the purely dialectical ones. In short, a man cannot possibly reason without first knowing what is reasoning and what is not reasoning, that is, without first knowing logic. Let us therefore quietly conclude that according to the very letter of the revealed Law, the philosopher is the only man who fulfils his religious duties and strictly obeys the prescriptions of Revelation.[1]

At this point, however, there arises a rather puzzling question. Were it true that the divine law enjoins us to seek God by the rational methods of philosophy, why should there be a supernatural revelation? In order to solve that problem, Averroës resorted to the Aristotelian distinction between the three main classes of arguments: the rhetorical, the dialectical and the necessary ones, and he suggested that all men be distributed among three corresponding classes: those who are apt to be persuaded by clever speech only, those that are more particularly open to dialectical probabilities, and those whom nothing can satisfy but the necessary demonstrations of the mathematicians and of the metaphysicians. Common people make up the whole population of the first class, which is by far the more crowded one. Such men are led by imag-

ination rather than by reason, and the only people
that are able to convince them are eloquent speak-
ers who know how to stir their feelings by appro-
priate arguments. All good preachers know how
to do it. You will not civilize a tribe of Bedouins
by teaching them metaphysics. If you want them
not to kill, not to plunder and not to drink, the
only thing for you to do is to appeal to their
imagination. Tell them, for instance, that there is
another world, where the good ones will enjoy
eternal fleshly pleasures, while the evil ones will
undergo eternal bodily punishments. The question
whether that is true or not is secondary in importance. The real question is, is it true that all
men should master their passions? We know it is,
and for very solid philosophical reasons. If that is
true, all men should be persuaded to do it; but nobody can be convinced by reasons which he cannot
understand, and that is the exact spot where the
necessity of religion appears in full: religion and
Revelation are nothing but philosophical truth
made acceptable to men whose imagination is
stronger than their reason.

Not so with the second class of men, that of the

dialectically minded ones. Materially speaking,
they believe just the same things as the rank and
file of the faithful, but they do not believe them
in the same way. In order to convince such men
it is not enough to appeal to their imagination and
to stir their emotions; they cannot be brought to
believe unless what they are asked to believe be
made at least believable in the light of natural
reason. In the first place, such men want to make
sure that nothing of what is taught by Revelation is at variance with verified scientific knowledge. In the second place, they want to be given
good reasons why they should believe this rather
than that. Fortunately, nothing is easier for us
than to find reasons in favor of what we already
believe. Such precisely is the proper function of
theology and of the theologians, not indeed to
demonstrate the truth of Revelation for faith
would no longer be faith if it could be rationally
proven; but to find out some dialectical justifica-
tions whereby Revelation will appear as at least
rationally probable, and even as more probable
than its contrary. There is no reason in the world
why such a thing should not be done. As a matter

of fact, theology has its own function to fulfil, for
if men of that type were forbidden to clothe their
beliefs in a more or less philosophical garb, they
would soon cease to believe, and not being able to
grasp real demonstrations, they would be left without either faith or philosophy. In short, such men
would have no principles to live by. Yet, true
philosophers cannot adopt such an attitude. Nothing short of necessary rational demonstrations will
quench their thirst for knowledge. The exceedingly
small number of thus minded men makes up the
third and highest class of human minds; but while
enjoying their aristocratic privilege, such men
should also be careful to discern and to respect
the solid nucleus of truth which lies hidden behind
the fancies of simple faith as well as behind the
dialectical probabilities of the theologians. For
instance, it is not true that the world has been
created out of nothing by a superworkman of
some sort, as the God of common faith is; philosophers will never accept that; yet they do know
that the world is hanging from a first cause in
both its existence and its intelligibility. Likewise,
it is simply not true that the first cause has created

the world in time; not a single one of the many
arguments whereby the theologians have sought to
prove that the world has had a beginning in time
is of any value and no true philosopher will ever
believe it; yet philosophers know by necessary
demonstration that the first cause is eternally
moving the world and necessarily begetting all that
which is in virtue of its infinite fecundity. It can
therefore be said, that these three different approaches to the same truth ultimately agree. What
the mob are holding as true by faith and what
the theologians are expressing in terms of dialectical probability, is nothing but philosophical
truth itself, adapted to the use of those lower
classes of minds. Faith is the only possible approach to rational truth for men of imagination;
theology is the next best thing to metaphysics for
a merely dialectical mind; but philosophy itself
is absolute truth, as established by the demonstrations of pure reason.[2]

Should all sensible men accept those conclusions, the perpetual strife that is raging between
simple believers, theologians and philosophers
would either come to an end or, at least, it would

boil down to something like the common frictions
of social life. No tragic conflicts between philosophers and theologians would ever arise, were it
not for the harmful inclination of so many amongst
us to mind somebody else's business. What is the
matter with the faithful is not that they are simple believers, but rather that they will play at
being theologians; and theologians themselves are
all right *qua* theologians, but you won't stop them
playing at being philosophers; and, to be quite
fair, let us add that philosophers are unimpeach-
able so long as they leave faith and theology alone,
but they won't do it. Yet they ought to, and
plain common sense should warn them off such
grounds. In point of fact, thoughtful metaphysicians never find themselves in conflict with any
conceivable revelation. Most of the time, their rational speculation will lead them to conclusions of
which Revelation says nothing; in such cases, there
can be no opposition between reason and Revelation. In the other cases, that is, when Revelation
and reason have to deal with the same problems,
they are bound either to agree or to disagree.
Assuming that they do agree, there is no conflict.

And assuming they disagree? Then the philosopher should not expect the faithful and the theologians to see his point; even though they would,
they simply could not do it. It is up to him to
make allowance for their own difficulties and to
respect, in both their beliefs and their dogmas, the
nucleus of philosophical truth that lies there. Let
the philosophers do this, and there will never be any
strife between reason and Revelation.[3]

This is how it may be. But with all due respect
to the perfect sincerity of Averroës' own inten-
tions, I fail to see how he could possibly hope to
placate the theologians by advocating such a pol-
icy. I am not quite sure that philosophers could
be easily persuaded to dismiss religion as being
but a crude approach to philosophy, but if a
philosopher starts teaching that there should be a
religion for the mob,[4] unless the man be a fool,
he cannot seriously hope to get away with it. There
is little consolation for theologians, in hearing it
said that Revelation is the next best thing to
philosophy, and that his own definition finally is:
a man who is not able to be a philosopher. As we
all know from bitter experience, some philosophers

do preach, but all preachers love to demonstrate.
Averroës himself knew it so well, that after ex-
plaining to his fellow philosophers the whole truth
about their superiority, he strongly advised them
to keep that truth to themselves. Nay, he even
advised them to keep philosophy to themselves, and
never either to preach it to the mob or to fight
for it against the theologians. The happy few
whom God has endowed with a philosophical mind
should content themselves with a solitary posses-
sion of rational truth. Let therefore philosophers
discuss such matters among themselves; let them
write down their conclusions in learned books,
which their technical character will protect against
the curiosity of the crowd; but don't let them
disturb the peace of simple minds with demonstrations that are above them. Thus understood, philosophy becomes an esoteric and truly secret science, so much so that Averroës wondered if it
were not a wise move officially to forbid the public
use of philosophical books. In point of fact, nothing wiser could be conceived by a man whose main
intention it was to establish a lasting peace between philosophers and theologians.[5]

The doctrinal position of Averroës was a very complex one and there is more in it than meets the eye. At first sight, it looks like a vicious attack against religion, and there is no denying that, from the point of view of the theologians it cannot bear any other interpretation. In the mind of Averroës himself however, things were far from being so simple. As most of the philosophers, he wanted social order, that he himself might philosophize in peace, and he knew full well that men could not possibly be civilized by merely being taught some abstract code of social ethics. In other words, Averroës did not consider religion as merely a rough approximation to philosophic truth. It was for him much more. It had a definite social function that could not be fulfilled by anything else, not even philosophy. Such is the exact meaning of the texts where he praises the Koran as a truly "miraculous" book. I see no reason not to take that word seriously. The more convinced Averroës was of the absolute superiority of philosophical knowledge, the more baffling must have been to him the existence of such a book, a book both wholly unphilosophical and much more effec-

tive than philosophy itself in raising barbarians
to the level of morality. In order to account for
that miracle, Averroës had finally to make room in
his doctrine for the fact that there are Prophets.
Prophets alone can perform miracles; but there
are miracles of deeds, as for instance the dividing
of the sea, which do not conclusively prove the
prophecy of any one, and there are miracles of
knowledge, which are the only conclusive proof of
it. The existence of Prophets is an empirical fact,
just as easily observable as that of traders or of
physicians. They have no proofs of the existence
of God, yet they know there is one, and when they
say it, everybody believes it. They never ask themselves whether man has a soul or not. They know
it. Moreover, as soon as they start preaching that
man has indeed a soul, and that man's happiness
ultimately hangs on his respect for such virtues as
justice and charity, the wildest barbarians begin
to listen, and behold something like real civilization actually sets in. To this you may object:
granted that the Prophets accomplished so much,
it remains a fact that what they say is not complete and absolute truth. But your very objection

shows how miraculous were the accomplishments of the Prophets. Had he happened to live in such times, a philosopher would have demonstrated the whole and absolute truth, and nobody would have listened to it. In point of fact, nobody does even in our own times. Because he is divinely inspired, on the contrary, a true Prophet, as Moses, Jesus Christ or Mohammed, knows exactly both what quantity of truth the common people can take in, and how to catch the ear of so restive an audience. As the Koran itself says (19:47): "Verily, if men and angels were purposely assembled, that they might produce a book like this Koran, they could not produce one like it." And the Koran is right, for nothing short of a divine inspiration could have produced it.[6]

As you can see, there is a long cry from the historical Averroës and the legendary author of the pamphlet later on circulated under his name: *The Three Impostors*. Far from considering Moses, Jesus and Mohammed as three cunning deceivers, he always respected them as three messengers of God unto mankind. But even that was not enough to placate theologians; what they wanted him to say was that the word of God is above any human word, be it that of the greatest philosophers themselves. Now Averroës had always maintained that philosophical truth was absolute truth, the Koran and its theological interpretations being nothing more to him than popular approaches to pure philosophy. No wonder then that he had to undergo severe persecutions. He died in Morocco, an exile from his native Spain, in the year 1198.

Difficult to maintain in a Moslem civilization, the position of Averroës was a strictly impossible one for his Latin disciples in the thirteenth century. First of all, they do not seem to have known the particular treatise which he had devoted to a detailed study of that problem. Next, those men who were acquainted with his commentaries upon Aristotle, and who received his conclusions as true, could not possibly teach them as an expression of the absolute truth. Not only because they were Christians, and all of them clerics, that is, churchmen, was this the case, but also because most of them were teaching in the thirteenth-century University of Paris, a clerical institution directly controlled by ecclesiastical authorities. A professor of

philosophy could not well be allowed to teach as
true in the Faculty of Arts of that University,
the very reverse of what his colleagues were teaching as true in the Faculty of Theology of the same
University. In a Church Institution, the only absolute truth had to be theological truth. Such being
the case, the problem of knowing whether or not
such men were acquainted with Averroës' own
treatment of the question is secondary in importance. Even knowing his complete answer to the
problem, they could not have made public use of
it. Hence their effort to work out such a position
on the question as would prove acceptable from
the point of view of the Church. In consequence of
this, there was the rise of a new spiritual family:
the Latin Averroists.

Among the many members of that family, I beg
to distinguish a first variety, which I cannot help
considering as entitled to our sincere sympathy.
For indeed those poor people found themselves in
sore straits. On the one side, they were good Christians and sincere believers. To them, it was beyond
a doubt that Christian Revelation was, not only
the truth, but the ultimate, supreme and absolute

truth. This reason in itself was sufficient to make it impossible for them to be Averroists in identically the same way as Averroës himself. On the other side, and this time as philosophers, this group failed to see how any one of Averroës' philosophical doctrines could be refuted. What were they to do in the many instances where their faith and their reason were at odds? For instance, their philosophy proved by necessary reasons that the world is eternal, perpetually moved by a self-thinking thought or mind, ruled from above by an intelligible necessity wholly indifferent to the destinies of individuals as such. In point of fact, the God of the Averroists does not even know that there are individuals, he knows only himself and that which is involved in his own necessity. Thus, knowing the human species, he is in no wise aware of the existence of those fleeting things, the individuals by which the eternal species is represented. Besides, as individuals, men have no intellect of their own; they do not think, they are merely thought into from above by a separate intellect, the same for the whole of mankind. Having no personal intellect, men can have no personal immortality, nor therefore can they hope for future rewards or fear eternal punishments in another life. Yet, at the same time when their reason was binding them to accept those conclusions, as philosophers, their faith was binding them to believe, as Christians, that the world has been freely created in time, by a God whose fatherly providence takes care of even the smallest among His Creatures; and if God so cares for every sparrow, what shall we say of man, who is of more value than many sparrows? Is not each of us endowed with a personal intellect of his own, responsible for each one of his thoughts as well as of his acts, and destined to live an immortal life of blessedness or of misery according to his own individual merits? In short, theology and philosophy were leading these men to conclusions that could neither be denied nor reconciled.

In order to free themselves from those contradictions, some among the Masters of Arts of the Parisian Faculty of Arts chose to declare that, having been appointed to teach philosophy, and nothing else, they would stick to their own job, which was to state the conclusions of philosophy such as necessarily follow from the principles of natural reason. True enough, their conclusions did not always agree with those of theology, but such was philosophy and they could not help it. Besides, it should be kept in mind that these professors would never tell their students, nor even think among themselves, that the conclusions of philosophy were true. They would say only this, that such conclusions were necessary from the point of view of natural reason; but what is human reason as compared with the wisdom and power of an infinite God? For instance, the very notion of a creation in time is a philosophical absurdity, but if we believe in God Almighty, why should not we also believe that, for such a God to create the world in time was not an impossibility? The same thing could be said everywhere. The conclusions of philosophy are at variance with the teaching of Revelation; let us therefore hold them as the *necessary* results of philosophical speculation, but, as Christians, let us believe that what Revelation says on such matters is *true;* thus, no contradiction will ever arise between philosophy and theology, or between Revelation and reason.

The doctrine of this first group of Latin Averroists is commonly called: the doctrine of the
twofold truth.[7] Philosophically justified as I think
it is, such a designation is not an historically correct one. Not a single one among those men would
have ever admitted that two sets of conclusions,
the one in philosophy, the other in theology, could
be, at one and the same time, both absolutely contradictory and absolutely true. There still are
many medieval writings to be discovered, but with
due reservation as to what could be found to the contrary in one of them, I can say that such a position
was a most unlikely one, and that I have not yet
been able to find a single medieval philosopher
professing the doctrine of the twofold truth. Their
actual position was a much less patently contradictory and a much less unthinkable one. As so
many men who cannot reconcile their reason with
their faith, and yet want them both, the Averroists
were keeping both philosophy and Revelation, with
a watertight separation between them. Why should
not a man feel sure that Averroës cannot be refuted, and yet believe that the most necessary
reasons fall short of the infinite wisdom of an all-

powerful God? I would not say that it is a logically safe position, nor a philosophically brilliant one, but the combination of blind fideism in theology with scepticism in philosophy is by no means an uncommon phenomenon in the history of human thought. I seem to hear one of those divided minds saying to himself: here is all that philosophy can say about God, man and human destiny; it is not much; yet that at least is conclusively proven and I cannot make philosophy say anything else. Were we living in a non-Christian world, such conclusions would not be merely necessary, they would also be truth. But God has spoken. We now know that what appears as necessary in the light of a finite reason is not necessarily true. Let us therefore take philosophy for what it is: the knowledge of what man would hold as true, if absolute truth had not been given to him by the divine Revelation. There have been men of that type in the thirteenth-century University of Paris; to the best of my knowledge, there is no reason whatever to suppose that Siger of Brabant and Boethius of Dacia for instance, both of them Averroists in philosophy, were not also perfectly sincere in their religious faith. Such, at least, was the personal conviction of Dante concerning Siger, for had he entertained the least suspicion about the sincerity of Siger's faith, he would not have put him in the fourth heaven of the Sun, together with Albertus Magnus and Thomas Aquinas.[8]

Besides that first group of Latin Averroists, there was another one, whose members were equally convinced that the philosophy of Averroës was the absolute truth, but felt no difficulty in reconciling it with their religious beliefs, because they had none. It is often said, and not without good reasons, that the civilization of the Middle Ages was an essentially religious one. Yet, even in the times of the Cathedrals and of the Crusades, not everybody was a saint; it would not even be correct to suppose that everybody was orthodox, and there are safe indications that confirmed unbelievers could be met on the streets of Paris and of Padua around the end of the thirteenth century. When such men were at the same time philosophers, the deism of Averroës was their natural philosophy. As to Revelation, they would profess, at least in words, absolute respect for its teachings, but none

of them would ever miss an opportunity to demonstrate by necessary reasons the very reverse of
what they were supposed to believe. Seen from
without, the members of this second group were
saying identically the same things as the members
of the first one, but their tone was different and,
cautious as they had to be, they usually found the
way to make themselves understood.

One of the best specimens of that variety was
undoubtedly the French philosopher John of
Jaudun, better known to historians as the associ-
ate of Marsiglio di Padoa in his campaign against
the temporal power of the Popes. Every time, in
his commentaries upon Aristotle, he reached one
of those critical points where his philosophy was
at variance with the conclusions of Christian theology, John never failed to restate his complete
submission to religious orthodoxy, but he usually
did it in a rather strange way. In some cases he
so obviously enjoys reminding us of all that which
he merely believes, and cannot prove, that one won-
ders what interests him more about those points,
that all of them should be believed, or that none
of them can be proved. Here is one of those texts:

"I believe and I firmly maintain that the substance of the soul is endowed with natural faculties whose activities are independent from all bodily organs. . . . Such faculties belong in a higher order than that of corporeal matter and far exceed its capacities. . . . And although the soul be united with matter, it nevertheless exercises an (intellectual) activity in which corporeal matter takes no part. All those properties of the soul belong to it truly, simply and absolutely, according to our own faith. And also that an immaterial soul can suffer from a material fire, and be reunited with its own body, after death, by order of the same God Who created it. On the other side, I would not undertake to demonstrate all that, but I think that such things should be believed by simple faith, as well as many others that are to be believed without demonstrative reasons, on the authority of Holy Writ and of miracles. Besides, this is why there is some merit in believing, for the theologians teach us, that there is no merit in believing that which reason can demonstrate." Most of the time, however, John of Jaudun would content himself with cracking some joke, which makes it difficult for his readers

to take seriously his most formal professions of
faith: "I do believe that that is true; but I cannot
prove it. Good luck to those who can!" And again:
"I say that God can do that, but how, I don't
know; God knows." Another time, after proving
at great length that the notion of creation is a
philosophical impossibility, John naturally adds
that we should nevertheless believe it. Of course,
says he, no philosopher ever thought of it, "And
no wonder, for it is impossible to reach the notion
of creation from the consideration of empirical
facts; nor is it possible to justify it by arguments
borrowed from sensible experience. And this is why
the Ancients, who used to draw their knowledge
from rational arguments verified by sensible experience, never succeeded in conceiving such a
mode of production." And here is the final stroke:
"Let it be added, that creation very seldom happens; there has never been but one, and that was
a very long time ago."[9] There was a slight touch
of Voltaire in John of Jaudun's irony; and yet,
his carefully worded jokes represent only what
could then be written; as is usually the case, much
more could be said.

In the year 1277, the Bishop of Paris, Etienne Tempier, solemnly condemned 219 propositions either borrowed from Averroistic writings, or expressing current Averroistic opinions. The list of those opinions is a sufficient proof of the fact that pure rationalism was steadily gaining ground around the end of the thirteenth century. Some of those propositions bluntly state, that: "there is no higher life than philosophical life" (*Prop.* 40); or that "there are no wisdoms in the world except that of the philosophers" (*Prop.* 154); and again: "that nothing should be believed, save only that which either is self-evident, or can be deduced from self-evident propositions" (*Prop.* 37). Such statements were just so many challenges to the primacy of Revelation, to the supremacy of Christian Wisdom and to the infallible truth of Revelation. Nor was that all, for some of those propositions went as far as saying that: "Christian Revelation is an obstacle to learning" (*Prop.* 175); and again, that: "one knows nothing more for knowing theology" (*Prop.* 153); and last, not the least, that "Theology rests upon fables" (*Prop.* 152).

Such an Averroism was not that of Averroës

himself, who, at least, entertained a sincere and deep respect for the moralizing power of revealed religions. It had little more in common with the attitude of Siger of Brabant and of Boethius of Dacia, in whose minds simple faith was enough to hold in check the boldest philosophical speculations. As a matter of fact, it was like nothing else in the past, but it anticipated the criticism of the religious dogmas which is a typical feature of the French eighteenth century. That the so-called Revelation is mythical in its origin is everywhere suggested in Fontenelle's *History of the Oracles* (1687) ; Fontenelle was a very prudent man; he was merely suggesting what he had in mind; but four centuries before him, some Averroists had clearly said it.

The existence of a medieval rationalism should never have been forgotten by those historians who investigate into the origins of the so-called modern rationalism, for indeed the Averroistic tradition forms an uninterrupted chain from the Masters of Arts of Paris and Padua, to the "Libertins" of the seventeenth and of the eighteenth centuries.[10] But it is still more important to remember it, for those who find it easy to sum up in some simple formula six centuries of medieval civilization. What the intellectual life of the Middle Ages might have been if Saint Augustine had never existed, I am not prepared to say; but I feel just as unable to fancy what might have become of it without Averroës and his Latin disciples, not only because they themselves would not have been there, but also because, had they not been there, the work of Saint Thomas Aquinas himself would not have been what it was.

# CHAPTER
# THREE

# III

---

# The Harmony of Reason
# and Revelation

DESPITE their radical opposition, the Theologism and the Rationalism of the thirteenth
century had at least one common feature; their
onesidedness. Theologism would maintain that
every part of Revelation should be understood,
while Rationalism would uphold the view that no
part of Revelation can be understood. The historical significance of Saint Thomas Aquinas rests
with the fact that he was the first medieval thinker
to go to the root of the difficulty. It would be quite
unfair to his predecessors to forget what they had
already done to clear up the problem. Moses
Maimonides, the greatest among the Jewish theologians, had clearly defined, in his *Guide for the
Perplexed*, the data for a complete solution of the
question. Ever since the beginning of the thir-

teenth century, there had been a growing tendency
among the Christian theologians themselves, to
draw a dividing line between the order of what we
believe and the order of what we know. Alexander
of Hales, Saint Bonaventura and still more evi-
dently Saint Albert the Great, had been most in-
sistent on the fundamental importance of that distinction. But the real reformer is not the man who
sees that a reform is needed; nor is he the man
who, in season and out of season, preaches the
necessity of that reform; the true reformer is the
man who achieves it.

Saint Thomas Aquinas was wonderfully equipped
to solve a problem of that kind, because it was a
problem of order. Now anyone who is at all
familiar with his work knows full well that he simply could not help putting everything in its proper
place. Each thing in its own place, a place for
each thing. Now, in everyday life, the problem of
putting a thing in its proper place is a compara-
tively simple one. It seldom amounts to more than
putting it always in the same place and remem-
bering where it is. Not so in philosophy, where
there is but one conceivable proper place for any

given thing. Unless you find it, that thing is lost, not in the usual sense that it is not to be found where you expected it to be, but in the much more radical sense that it is no longer to be found any-where. Out of its proper place, the thing simply cannot exist at all. For indeed, the place of each thing is determined there by its own essence, and unless you know first what the thing is you shall never be able to define its relations to what it is not.

When stated as an abstract principle, the gen-eral idea of such a method is easy enough to under-stand; but nobody can apply it to concrete cases unless he be possessed of two intellectual qualities, whose combination in the same mind is rather rare: a perfect intellectual modesty and an almost reck-less intellectual audacity. Now Saint Thomas Aquinas had both in an uncommonly high degree. He had intellectual modesty, because he always began by accepting things just as they were. Thomas Aquinas never expected that things would conform themselves to his own definitions of them; quite the reverse, what he would call the true knowledge of a thing was the adequate intellectual expression of the thing such as it is in itself. But he had also intellectual audacity, for, after accepting a thing such as it was, he would insist on dealing with it according to its own nature, and he would do it fearlessly, without compromise. In the present case, the trouble was that some theologians wanted to theologize in philosophy, whereas some philosophers wanted to philosophize in theology. Consequently, the only way to bring that strife to a close was for Saint Thomas Aquinas to handle philosophical problems as a philosopher and theological problems as a theologian.

In order to clear up the difficulty, let us begin by defining the proper nature of religious faith. To have faith is to assent to something because it is revealed by God. And now, what is it to have science? It is to assent to something which we perceive as true in the natural light of reason. The essential difference between these two distinct orders of assent should be carefully kept in mind by anybody dealing with the relations of Reason and Revelation. I know by reason that something is true because *I see* that it is true; but I believe that something is true because *God has said it*. In those two cases the cause of my assent is spe-

cifically different, consequently science and faith
should be held as two specifically different kinds
of assent.

If they are two distinct species of knowledge, we
should never ask one of them to fulfil what is the
proper function of the other. We should never
do it for the simple reason that, since they are
specifically distinct, one of them cannot possibly
be the other one. For instance, I cannot possibly
ask you to believe that I am here; you cannot
believe it, because you see it. On the other hand,
I cannot cause you to see that I am now interpret-
ing for you the fifth article of the second section
of the second Part of the *Summa Theologica* of
Saint Thomas Aquinas. I can only ask you to believe it. Later on, if you check up my reference,
you will see whether I was right or wrong in quoting it; and then you will know whether I was right
or wrong, but it will become impossible for you
to believe it. Now the same distinction should apply
to the problem of reason and Revelation. According to its very definition, faith implies assent of
the intellect to that which the intellect does not
see to be true, either as one of the first principles,

or as one of their necessary conclusions. Consequently, an act of faith cannot be caused by a rational evidence, but entails an intervention of the will. On the contrary, in scientific knowledge, my assent is sufficiently and completely determined by its very object. Whence there follows that, in Thomas Aquinas' own words, since "it is impossible that one and the same thing should be believed and seen by the same person, . . . it is equally impossible for one and the same thing to be an object of science and of belief for the same person." In short, one and the same thing cannot be at one and the same time both an object of science and an object of faith.   •

When we read those lines, what they say seems to be pretty obvious; and, in a way, it was; yet those simple statements are a landmark in the history of western thought. By taking such a stand, Thomas Aquinas was challenging the distinction more or less confusedly implied in so many theologies, between the simple faith of common people, and the enlightened faith of the *meliores*, who add to faith its understanding.[1] It is typical of Saint Thomas Aquinas that he could not tolerate even

the shadow of such a confusion: "that which is
proposed to be believed equally by all is unknown
by all as an object of science: such are the things
which are of faith simply." Consequently, if we
are dealing with those things which are essentially
of faith, it becomes absurd to draw any distinction
between the mass of the simple believers and the
aristocracy of those who add to the same faith its
understanding. As believers, all Christians are in
the same predicament, for all of them agree as to
what they believe, and none of them has any scientific knowledge of it.

What then should we answer, when great theologians, who sometimes are also great saints, en-
join us to accept their reasons as necessary demonstrations of what we hold as true by faith?
Simply that it cannot be done. The authority of
so high a saint and of so great a theologian as
Saint Anselm himself has absolutely nothing to
do with the question. In fact, "the reasons em-
ployed by holy men to prove things that are of
faith are not demonstrations." And why? Because
they cannot be. If that which they pretend to
demonstrate were really demonstrated, it would

become scientifically known and therefore could no longer be believed.[2]

Saint Thomas did not content himself with a mere abstract statement of his general answer to the question, he applied it to the solution of many particular problems. And no wonder, for in all those cases the very nature of Revelation, of faith and of theology itself was at stake. In its own way, theology itself is a science, whose conclusions necessarily follow from their principles; but those principles are articles of faith, and faith itself is an assent to the word of God accepted as word of God. Were we to say, on the contrary, that there are necessary demonstrations of the revealed truth, we could no longer believe in it, there would be no articles of faith, no principles of theological reasoning, no theology conceived as a distinct order of knowledge. In other words, revealed theology, or the theology of Revelation, would disappear as religious knowledge; what would be left in its place would be natural theology, that is to say, metaphysics.

Such was the fundamental reason why Saint Thomas Aquinas never failed to stress the tran-

REASON AND REVELATION 77

scendent nature and incomparable dignity of the
word of God every time he could find some appro-
priate occasion to do it. If it is of the essence of
an article of faith to rest upon divine authority
alone, its would-be demonstrations cannot possibly
be necessary demonstrations. Now our faith in
Revelation should not be a merely natural assent
to some rational probability. When something is
rationally probable, its contrary also is rationally
probable. It is but an opinion. Religious faith is
not an opinion. It is the unshakable certitude that
God has spoken, and that what God has said is
true, even though we do not understand it. Hence
Thomas Aquinas' repeated warnings not to over-
rate the value of such probabilities, lest, as he himself says, "the Catholic faith seem to be founded
on empty reasonings, and not, as it is, on the most
solid teaching of God."[3] And again: "And it is
useful to consider this, lest anyone, presuming to
demonstrate what is of faith, should bring forward
reasons that are not cogent, so as to give occasion
to unbelievers to laugh, and to think that such
are the grounds on which we believe things that are
of faith."[4]

By thus excluding from theology all necessary
demonstrations of purely rational nature, Thomas
Aquinas was cutting loose from the theologism of
the early Middle Ages. From now on, and up to
our own days, there have always been men to maintain that Revelation is a self-sufficient and self-
contained order of truth, whose ultimate founda-
tion is divine authority alone and not the natural
light of reason. This, however, should immediately
be added, that the specific distinction introduced
by Thomas Aquinas between faith and rational
knowledge was not understood by him as a separation, still less as an Averroistic opposition. To
those professors of philosophy who deemed it ex-
pedient to state their conclusions as necessary, but
not as true, Thomas Aquinas objected that their
position was an impossible one. In describing their
authentic attitude, we had to stress the fact that
no Averroist could be quoted as having said that
he believed by faith as true the very reverse of
what he knew by necessary reasons to be true. We
even added that, psychologically speaking, theirs
was by no means an inconceivable attitude. But
Thomas Aquinas was right in pointing to the fact

that their philosophical position involved a latent absurdity.

Just as Averroës himself, Thomas Aquinas felt convinced that nothing should enter the texture of metaphysical knowledge save only rational and necessary demonstrations. For the same reason, he even agreed with Averroës that the so-called necessary reasons of so many theologians were mere dialectical probabilities. As he once said of such arguments, they never convince anyone unless he already believes what they are supposed to prove. Moreover, Thomas Aquinas had in common with Averroës an immense admiration for Aristotle, whose fundamental principles he certainly identified with those of natural reason itself. As to Averroës, he was to Thomas Aquinas what he was to everybody else in the Middle Ages: the Commentator *par excellence*. Yet Saint Thomas never considered Averroës as a faultless interpreter of Aristotle, nor Aristotle himself as an infallible philosopher. The attitude of the Latin Averroists was an altogether different one. Whereas Thomas Aquinas would follow Aristotle when he was right, but no further, and because he was right, but on

no other ground, the Averröists would consider
Averroës, Aristotle and human reason, as three
different words for one and the same thing. That
surprising attitude does not account only for the
philosophical sterility of their school as a whole,
but also for the passive resignation of some of them
between the antinomies of Christian faith and of
natural reason. Convinced, as they were, that not
a word could be altered in the works of Averroës
without wrecking philosophy itself, they could do
but one of two things: either drop their religious
beliefs, in which case there was nothing left to
harmonize, or else accept contradiction as a normal
condition of the human mind.

Saint Thomas Aquinas did his very best to convince them that their ill-guided devotion to the
letter of what they took to be philosophy was
indeed destructive of philosophy. To say that the
conclusions of Averroës were rationally necessary,
but not necessarily true, was to empty the word
"truth" of all meaning. If that which appears as
necessary in the light of natural reason cannot
be posited as true, what else will be posited as
true in philosophy? That which is not contradicted

by Revelation? But if rational evidence falls short
of the truth in a single case it becomes meaning-
less in all the others. Hence Saint Thomas' own
interpretation and refutation of their position. If
what is rationally necessary is thereby necessarily
true, those Averroists were actually teaching a
doctrine of the twofold truth; they were main-
taining as simultaneously true two sets of contradictory propositions.

By bringing together the results of the two
distinct criticisms directed by Thomas Aquinas
against the theologism of Saint Anselm and the
Averroism of Siger de Brabant, we begin to discern the general features of a third position on
the problem, as well as of a third spiritual family,
that of the Thomists. All its members will grant
that there is a true Revelation: the Christian Revelation. They grant it, but they do not take it for
granted. No man would ever admit that God has
spoken, unless he had solid proofs of the fact.
Such proofs are to be found in history, where the
miracles of God, and quite especially the greatest
of all: the life and growth of His Church, prove
His presence, the truth of His doctrine and the

permanence of His inspiration. If truly God has
spoken, His Revelation must needs be true, and it
is necessary for us to believe it. For this is the
proper aim and scope of Revelation to provide all
men, philosophers or not, with such a knowledge
of God, of man and of his destiny, as is required
for their eternal salvation. Now, that knowledge
itself is made up of several different elements,
among which two main classes should be carefully
distinguished. The first one comprises a certain
number of revealed truths which, though they be
revealed, are nevertheless attainable by reason
alone. Such are, for instance, the existence of God
and His essential attributes, or the existence of
the human soul and its immortality. Why did God
reveal to men even some truths which natural reason could attain? Because very few men are metaphysicians, whereas all men need to be saved. By
revealing them to mankind, God has enabled each
of us to know the whole saving truth immediately,
with absolute certitude and in its perfect purity.[5]
Yet, any part of Revelation which is attainable by
natural reason should be considered rather as a
necessary presupposition to matters of faith than

as an article of faith properly said.[6] Only those
men who cannot see its truth in the light of reason
are held in conscience to accept it by simple faith.
The second group of revealed truths contains all
the articles of faith properly said, that is to say,
all that part of the Revelation which surpasses the
whole range of human reason. Such are, for instance, the Trinity, the Incarnation and the Redemption. No philosophical speculation can give
any necessary reason in favor of any truth of that
kind; no philosophical conclusions can be deduced
from any articles of faith, for they are believed
principles of equally believed theological conse-
quences, not intelligible principles of demonstrated
rational conclusions. Yet, if reason cannot prove
them to be true, it cannot either prove them to
be false. Quite the reverse. To any sincere believer who is at the same time a true philosopher,
the slightest opposition between his faith and his
reason is a sure sign that something is the matter
with his philosophy. For indeed faith is not a principle of philosophical knowledge, but it is a safe
guide to rational truth and an infallible warning
against philosophical error. A man who does not

like to believe what he can know, and who never
pretends to know what can be but believed, and yet
a man whose faith and knowledge grow into an
organic unity because they both spring from the
same divine source, such is, if not the portrait, at
least a sketch of the typical member of the Thomist
family. Cajetan and John of Saint Thomas were
men of that type and still today one of its finest
specimens can be found amongst us, in the person
of M. Jacques Maritain.

Had it been given to Thomas Aquinas to convince, if not his own contemporaries, at least his
immediate successors, the intellectual and moral
crisis would have soon come to a close, and the
whole history of western thought would have been
different from what it was. Unfortunately, the net
result of Averroës' influence was to breed in the
minds of the theologians a growing mistrust for
philosophy. If that was natural reason, Revelation would be better off without its help than with
it. Hence, in even the greatest among the late medieval philosophers and theologians, an increasing
tendency to ascribe to faith alone, not only what
Thomas Aquinas would call the articles of faith

properly said, but even what we saw him define as
rational preambles to matters of faith. It thus
came to pass that the list of the revealed truths
that can be either believed, or proven, was steadily
growing shorter and shorter to the point of shrivel-
ling into nothingness. A typical instance of that
historical phenomenon can be found, within the
Thomist school itself, in the person of no less a
man than Cardinal Cajetan, one of the greatest
commentators of Saint Thomas Aquinas. Cajetan
entertained grave doubts as to the power of natural
reason to demonstrate the immortality of the soul,
and consequently the existence of future rewards
and punishments. But Cajetan was writing in the
sixteenth century and, by that time, the other
theological schools had already followed the same
road up to its very end.

As early as the last years of the thirteenth century, Duns Scotus had considerably increased the
list of those revealed truths which a Christian
should believe, but cannot prove. At the end of
his treatise *On the First Principle*, Duns Scotus
expressly states that the all-powerfulness of God,
His immensity, His omnipresence, His providence,

His justice and His *miséricord* towards all creatures, but especially towards man, are as many
beliefs not susceptible of rational demonstration.
Should the famous *Theoremata* be ascribed to him,
the list of those undemonstrable propositions would
become a considerably longer one. But the point
is immaterial to the problem at stake. Whoever
wrote the *Theoremata*, often ascribed to Duns
Scotus, the fact remains that their author listed
among the undemonstrable propositions, besides
the preceding ones, the unicity of God, the creation of the world out of nothingness, and its present conservation by the same God who once created
it. True enough, all such articles of faith can
be proved in theology by rational and necessary
demonstrations; that is, they can be proved pro-
vided they be believed first; but philosophical reason alone utterly fails to prove them.

The next step along the same line was taken by
the English Franciscan, William of Ockham, in the
first third of the fourteenth century. A bitter
opponent of Duns Scotus, Ockham always maintained that absolutely nothing could be proved
about God in the light of natural reason, not even

His existence. To him, as to Averröes, what reason can say concerning theological matters never goes beyond the order of mere dialectical probability. It is indeed probable that there is a God, who created the heaven and the earth; it is also probable that man has been endowed by God with a soul, and that, being an uncorporeal substance, that soul is immortal. Ockham would look at such propositions not only as probable ones, but as distinctly more probable than their contraries. Yet, none of them could be demonstrated in philosophy, and consequently, in spite of all that Anselm and Duns Scotus could say to the contrary, they could not be demonstrated even in theology. In short, they could not be demonstrated at all.

The influence of Ockham is everywhere present in the fourteenth century; it progressively invaded Oxford, Paris, and practically all the European universities. Some would profess it, others would refute it, but nobody was allowed to ignore it. The late Middle Ages were then called upon to witness the total wreck of both scholastic philosophy and scholastic theology as the necessary upshot of the final divorce of reason and Revela-

tion. Granted that not a single one of the revealed truths could possibly be justified by natural
reason, why should pious souls have paid the slightest attention to philosophy? It could do no good,
but it could do infinite harm to most of those who
studied it. I wonder how many among the readers
of the *Imitation of Christ* are conscious of reading
a late medieval protest against the vanity of all
philosophy? Very few, I suppose, and I would
not blame the other ones, for the true greatness of
the book does not lie there. Yet, whoever he was,
the author of that famous treatise was certainly
no great admirer of philosophers, nor even of theologians. "If you knew the whole Bible by heart,"
he says in the very first chapter of his book, "and
the sayings of all the philosophers, what would
that profit you without the love of God and grace?
Vanity of vanities, all is vanity, save to love God
and to serve Him only." (*Imit.* I: 1, 10–11.) Again,
"The time shall come when the Teacher of teachers,
Christ, the Lord of Angels, shall appear to hear
the lessons of all, that is, to examine the consciences
of each one; and then He shall search Jerusalem
with candles, and the hidden things of darkness

shall be manifest, and the arguing of men's tongues shall be silent. I am he who exalteth in a moment the humble mind, to comprehend more reasonings of the eternal truth than if one had studied ten years in the schools." (*Imit*. III:43, 10–11.)[7]

It is a blessing for all of us that the problem of who wrote the *Imitation* does not fall within the scope of the present inquiry. Several different writers have been made responsible for that book, and I happen to be personally acquainted with four historians who have discovered its true author; unfortunately, no two of them have discovered the same. But I hasten to add that, in so far as I can see, many other names have been quoted or could be quoted without absurdity. Here again we find ourselves confronted with a more or less definite group of kindred minds, whose answers to the problem of faith and reason were substantially the same. As early as the fifteenth century their common attitude had already been given a name: the *Moderna devotio*, that is, the modern, or new devotion. All the best historians of that movement agree at least on this, that it expressed a feeling of lassitude, after the failure of so many philosophers and

theologians to achieve anything like a commonly
received truth. Duns Scotus had disagreed with
Thomas Aquinas and Ockham had disagreed with
Duns Scotus. Whom should one believe? True
enough, the masters of mystical life had found a
way out of that maze in what they called the union
of the soul with God. But had they really found
it? Meister Eckhart's doctrine had been condemned
by Pope John XXII in 1329; John Ruysbroeck
was being accused of Averroism by John Gerson,
who himself was not without a smacking of Occam-
ism. Many fourteenth-century Christians were
simply fed up with the whole business. They had
no use for speculative theology, they would not
loose themselves into the obscure and unsafe mysteries of mystical union; what they wanted was
straight practical Christian life, and nothing else.
Gehrard Groote (Gerritt Groot) was prompted by
such a motive when, in 1381, he established in
Deventer the fraternity of the *Brethren of the
Common Life*. Gehrard Groote is one of the possible authors of the *Imitation of Christ*. Near Deventer, and in close relations with the *Brethren of
the Common Life*, was the monastery of the Canons

Regular of Windesheim; one of its Priors, John Vos de Huesden, has left us a "conférence" whose doctrine closely resembles that of the *Imitation*. One of the most popular candidates to the title, Thomas à Kempis, had been educated at Deventer.[8] But it should not be forgotten that though the odds seem now to be against him, John Gerson has long been a favorite. Now, when historians want to describe his fundamental attitude, what do they call it? A "reaction from excessive speculation."[9] From whatever angle we may choose to consider the then existing situation, nothing can be seen there, save only lassitude and discouragement.

When the best minds began to despair of harmonizing the teachings of Christian Revelation with those of philosophy, the end of the Middle Ages was at hand. In 1475, a twelve-year-old boy entered the school of the *Brethren of the Common Life*. His name was Desiderius Erasmus. One of the greatest among the great figures of the Renaissance, Erasmus was nevertheless a perfect expression of the fourteenth-century reaction against both scholastic philosophy and scholastic theology. Or rather, what is usually considered as a typical

feature of the early Renaissance is but the normal
development of a tendency, probably as old as
Christianity itself, but whose immediate origins are
to be found way back in the first years of the
fourteenth century. 'Away with philosophy,' and
'Back to the Gospel,' such was, in a nutshell, the
doctrine of Erasmus in his *Paraclesis* (1516), and
in his *Ratio seu methodus perveniendi ad veram
philosophiam* (1518). A long time before him,
Petrarch had already said pretty much the same
thing. What we call the "Christian humanism" of
the Renaissance owes its final triumph to the
marvellous talent of Erasmus; but the medieval
founders of the *New Devotion* had laid down the
very premises whence their pupil Erasmus was to
draw his conclusions.

Nor is that all. Among the typical expressions of
the medieval reaction from excessive speculation,
special mention should be made of another anony-
mous treatise, written by some German theologian
in the course of the fourteenth century: the so-
called *Theologia deutsch*, that is, a *German Theology*.[10] Martin Luther published it for the first
time in 1516, then again in 1518, this time with

an enthusiastic Preface, where he went as far as
saying: "I declare that I have not found any book,
except the Bible and Saint Augustine, which has
taught me more of the meaning of God, Christ,
man, and everything."[11] Even taking into account
the lack of aptness at understatement so often
betrayed by Luther's writings, the fact remains
that his discovery of the *Theologia deutsch* marks
an important date in his religious evolution. What
delighted him in that treatise was its complete in-
difference to speculative theology. Now Luther himself was well trained in scholastic theology[12] but
he hated it as being destructive of simple faith and
therefore of Christianity itself. It is significant that
in 1517, that is, just a year after the publishing of
the *German Theology*, Luther entrusted one of his
students with the task of publicly disputing against
scholastic theology. In this important document,
the bitterness of innumerable priests, monks,
preachers and University professors that, for two
centuries at least, had been accumulating against
scholastic philosophy, found at last its complete
expression. "The whole of Aristotle," Luther says,
"is to theology as darkness is to light. Against

Scholasticism." And to those who go on repeating, "Nobody becomes a theologian without Aristotle," Luther answers: "Quite the reverse: only without Aristotle can we become theologians."[13]

If the *New Devotion* can be truly considered as having, if not caused, at least occasioned, the Lutheran spirituality on the one side and the Christian humanism of Erasmus on the other side, its significance for the history of the Renaissance, and therefore of modern times themselves, should no longer be neglected by any thoughtful historian. Now, the rise of that *New Devotion* itself was largely ascribable to the disruption of the Thomistic synthesis under the lasting pressure of Averroës and of the Latin Averroists. Thus understood, the history of western thought from the thirteenth up to the sixteenth centuries begins to assume some sort of intelligibility. What was new at the times of the Renaissance still appears as having then been new, but we see it rooted in a medieval past by which alone it can be explained. After the Reformers and the Humanists, the men of the sixteenth century found themselves confronted with a theology without philosophy: the *positive* or *modern* phi-

losophy of Fr. de Vitoria and of M. Cano; and a
philosophy without theology: the purely rational
speculation of R. Descartes and of Francis Bacon.
In the light of our previous analyses, how could we
fail to perceive that the so-called modern conditions
of both theology and philosophy were the practically unavoidable upshot of at least two centuries
of medieval speculation? For indeed, between the
harmony of faith and reason as achieved by
Thomas Aquinas and their radical divorce, there
was no room left for an intermediate position.

If it be true that in spite of its slow and
fluctuating evolution the history of ideas is determined from within by the internal necessity of ideas
themselves, the conclusions of our inquiry should
exhibit a more than historical value. Wherever
and whenever the problem of the relations of faith
and reason may happen to be asked, the abstract
conditions of its solution are bound to remain the
same. Now it should not be forgotten that, even
in our own days, the question is very far from being
out of date. If, thirty years ago, anybody had asked
himself the question: Who are the two leading
philosophers of our own times? his answer would

have been: W. James and H. Bergson. In point of fact, we learn from Professor R. B. Perry's admirable biography of W. James, that "the first conjunction of those two luminaries took place on May 28, 1905." We know from Bergson himself how the two great thinkers greeted one another: "I believe that we did indeed say '*Bonjour,*' but that was all; there were several instants of silence, and straightway he asked me how I envisaged the problem of religion."[14]

The *Varieties of Religious Experience* and the *Twofold Sources of Ethics and Religion* are there, as irrecusable witnesses to their seriousness of purpose. It would be neither intelligent nor fair to deal in five minutes with such philosophical masterpieces; but I cannot help feeling that both books would be still greater than they actually are if their conclusions had taken into account seven centuries of historical experience. It is psychologically interesting to know that it does one good to *believe* there is a God; but that is not at all what the believer believes; what he actually believes is, that there *is* a God. The problem of religion requires that there is some being to which we must be bound;

and the problem of Revelation requires that there
is some divinely made statement to which we must
bow. I am not at all denying the intrinsic validity
of the other attitudes, but I beg to stress the fact
that, useful and instructive as they may prove to
be, they finally leave out the religious problem itself. Indeed, they cannot even ask it. After reading
W. James, I still want to know if my religious experience is an experience of God, or an experience
of myself. For in both cases there can be a psy-
chological religious experience, but in the first case
only can there be a religion. Similarly, I can follow
Bergson in his description of mystical intuition as
a source of religious life, but even after reading
him, I am still wondering what the nature of that
intuition actually is. Is it a self-sufficient intuition
of an object which may also be the object of religious faith, or is it an experience in faith and
through faith of the God in whom we believe?

Here again, the matter is an important one, and
the solution is bound to qualify all that can be said
on that question. This is so true, that despite their
cleverness in avoiding, as unphilosophical, the
problem of an historical Revelation of God to men,

even contemporary philosophers are driven back to
it by the very nature of the question. How indeed
could they help it? The very meaning of the problem itself is at stake. As Bergson himself says:
"At the origin of Christianity, there is Christ."[15]
Likewise, after painstakingly describing in his
book what he calls the "inner witness of the Holy
Spirit," Rudolf Otto warns us, in his last page,
that above that witness, there is the Prophet, and
that, above the Prophet, there is such a one as is
more than Prophet. The four last words of the book
at last tell us who he is: "He is the Son."[16]

There, I think, the real question begins. Knowing, as we do, that He who is more than Prophet has
spoken, what are we to do with His message? If
what His message says does at times escape the
grasp of natural reason, what is natural reason
going to say about it? Once we have reached that
point, God can no longer be conceived by us as a
mere "wholly other" to which our *a priori* cate-
gory of the "Numinous" bears witness; the Son
also is a witness, and He has said who the Father is.
That, at last, is a Revelation worthy of the name:
not our own revelation of God to ourselves, but the

Revelation of God Himself to us. Such are the only conceivable terms of the real problem, and since they are identically the same as those of the medieval problem, it would be a wise thing to do, for any one interested in solving it, to become acquainted with the writings of medieval theologians. For there is at least one thing that we still can learn from them concerning that question, and this is the correct way to ask it. So long as we ask no more than to harmonize our own religious feelings with our private impression of philosophical knowledge, we are still very far from encountering the real difficulty. If, on the contrary, we learn from medieval theologians what is faith in an objective truth and what is an objective philosophical knowledge, we shall find ourselves possessed of both a Revelation and a Reason. There then will be something to harmonize, and anyone attempting to do it will end at last in meeting the real problem. But he can scarcely avoid meeting Saint Thomas Aquinas.

# NOTES

# Notes

[ Pp. 8-13 ]

## CHAPTER I

(1) As a general introduction to the question, see
TH. HEITZ, *Essai historique sur les rapports entre la
philosophie et la foi, de Bérenger de Tours à saint
Thomas d'Aquin*, Gabalda, Paris, 1909. See also M.
GRABMANN, *Die Geschichte der scholastischen Methode*,
Herder, Freiburg i. Br., 2 vols., 1909. E. GILSON, *The
Spirit of Mediæval Philosophy*, transl. by A. H. C.
Downes, Scribner, New York, 1936. The best reference
book for general information concerning medieval philos-
ophers, their works, lives and doctrines, is FRIED. UEBER-
WEGS, *Grundriss der Geschichte der Philosophie*, Pt. II:
*Die patristische und scholastische Philosophie*, edit. by
B. Geyer, Mittler, Berlin, 1928. The best summary of
the history of medieval theology is that of M. GRABMANN,
*Die Geschichte der Katholischen Theologie seit dem
Ausgang der Väterzeit*, Herder, Freiburg i. Br., 1933;
pp. 1–133.

(2) TERTULLIAN, *On Prescription against Heretics*,
Ch. VII; in *The Ante-Nicene Fathers*, Buffalo, 1887;
Vol. III, p. 246. Cf. J. LÖRTZ, *Tertullian ab Apologet*,
Aschendorff, Münster i. Westf., 1927. For an easily avail-
able text, see TERTULLIAN, *On the Testimony of the Soul*
and *On the 'Prescription' of Heretics*, transl. by T. H.
Bindley, S.P.C.K., London, 1914.

(3) TATIAN, *Address to the Greeks*, in *The Ante-
Nicene Fathers*, Buffalo, 1885; Vol. II, Ch. II, p. 65,
and Ch. XXXII, p. 78. Cf. A. PUECH, *Recherches sur
le Discours aux Grecs de Tatien*, F. Alcan, Paris, 1903.

(4) SAINT BERNARD, *op. cit.*, in *St. Bernard's Sermons
for the seasons and principal festivals of the year*, transl.
by a Priest of Mount Melleray, Dublin, Browne and

Nolan, 1923; Vol. II, pp. 310 & 311. Cf. E. GILSON, *La
théologie mystique de saint Bernard,* J. Vrin, Paris, 1934.

(5) On Peter Damiani, see J. A. ENDRES, *Petrus
Damiani und die weltliche Wissenschaft,* Aschendorff,
Münster i. Westf., 1910. Cf. E. GILSON, *Études de
philosophie médiévale,* Strasbourg, 1921; pp. 31–38.

(6) I am quoting from the rhythmical rendering, in
ANNE MACDONELL, *Sons of Francis,* London, J. M. Dent,
and N. Y., G. P. Putnam's Sons, 1902; p. 369. More texts
to the same effect will be found in the same chapter,
pp. 354–386.

(7) The passage is translated in: J. SIGHART, *Albert
the Great, O.P., his Life and Scholastic Labours,* London,
R. Washbourne, 1876; Ch. VII, pp. 85–86. Even as late
as the XVIIth century, Francis Bacon had to take into
account the existence and activity of those more zealous
than enlightened theologians, as can be seen from his book
*On the Advancement of Learning,* I, 2. The "funda-
mentalists" are an undying race; like the Jebusites, they
cannot be exterminated.
     Cf. GILB. MURRAY, *Five Stages of Greek Religion,*
Columbia Univ. Press, 1925.

(8) SAINT AUGUSTINE, *On the Gospel of Saint John,*
XXIX, 6; in *Homilies on the Gospel of St. John,* transl.
by H. Browne, J. H. Parker (A Library of Fathers),
Oxford, 1848; Vol. I, p. 440.

(9) SAINT AUGUSTINE, *On free will,* II, 2, 6; as translated in E. PRZYWARA, *An Augustine Synthesis,* N. Y.,
Sheed and Ward, 1936; pp. 58–59. Other texts of Augustine on the same subject will be found in the same book,
pp. 41–58: *From understanding to faith;* and pp. 58–67:
*From faith to understanding.* Cf. J. MARITAIN, *St. Augustine and St. Thomas Aquinas,* transl. by Fr. Leonard, in
*A Monument to Saint Augustine,* Sheed and Ward, London, 1930, pp. 199–223.

(10) THOMAS AQUINAS, *Summa Theologica,* Pt. I, qu.
84, art. 5, Answer; transl. by the Fathers of the English

Dominican Province, p. 171: "Consequently whenever Augustine, who was imbued with the doctrines of the Platonists . . ." etc.

(11) E. Gilson, *Introduction à l'étude de saint Augustin*, J. Vrin, Paris, 1929, pp. 86–137. Other approaches to the same problem will be found in J. Hessen, *Augustins Metaphysik der Erkenntnis*, F. Dümmler, Berlin, 1931; and F. Cayré, *La contemplation augustinienne*, A. Blot, Paris, 1927.

(12) Saint Anselm, *Monologium*, Preface; transl. by S. N. Deane, The Open Court Co., Chicago, 1935, p. 36; and *Proslogium*, Preface, pp. 6–7.

(13) Gaunilo, *Liber pro insipiente, ibid*. Cf. the text and its French translation in A. Koyré, *St. Anselme de Canterbéry, Fides quaerens intellectum*, J. Vrin, Paris, 1930.

(14) Saint Anselm, *Cur Deus homo*, Preface; we are partly following S. N. Deane's translation, pp. 177–178.

(15) Roger Bacon, *Opus majus*, Pt. IV, Dist. 1, Ch. 1; in R. B. Burke's translation, Philadelphia, Univ. of Pennsylvania Press, 1928; Vol. I, pp. 123–124.

(16) Roger Bacon, *Opus majus*, Pt. IV, Dist. 4: *The application of mathematics to sacred subjects;* Vol. I, pp. 238–242.

(17) Roger Bacon, *Opus majus*, Pt. VI, Ch. 2; Vol. II, pp. 586–587. On that important aspect of Bacon's doctrine, see the remarkable book of R. Carton, *L'expérience mystique de l'illumination intérieure chez Roger Bacon*, J. Vrin, Paris, 1924.

(18) Cf. the shorter redaction of Lull's *Ars magna*, published by Carm. Ottaviano, *L'Ars compendiosa de R. Lulle*, J. Vrin, Paris, 1930.

(19) E. A. Peers, *Ramon Lull, a Biography*, S.P.C.K., London, 1929; pp. 312–313. A very valuable introduction to the study of Lull.

## CHAPTER II

(1) The arabic text of the *Theology of Aristotle* has been published and translated into German, by FR. DIETERICI, *Die sogenannte Theologie des Aristoteles aus arabischen Handschriften zum erstenmal herausgegeben;* J. C. Hinrich, Leipzig, 1882.

The gothic editions of Avicenna are very difficult to find; but there is an easily available abridgment of his *Metaphysics,* written by Avicenna himself, and translated into Latin by NEM. CARAME, *Avicennae Metaphysices Compendium,* Pontif. Inst. Orient. Stud., Rome; no date. Another, still more complete restatement of Avicenna's philosophy can be found in the Latin medieval translation of *Algazel's Metaphysics, a Mediæval Translation,* edit. by J. T. Muckle, Sheed and Ward, New York, 1933. Cf. M. HORTEN, *Die Metaphysik Avicennas, enthaltend die Metaphysik, Theologie, Kosmologie und Ethic, übersetzt und erlautert;* R. Haupt, Halle a.S. und New York, 1907. D. J. SALIBA, *Étude sur la métaphysique d'Avicenne,* Presses Universitaires, Paris, 1926.

ASIN PALACIOS, *Algazel: Dogmatica, moral, ascetica* (Coleccion de estudios arab., Vol. VI), Comas, Zaragoza, 1901. CARRA DE VAUX, *Gazali,* F. Alcan, Paris, 1902.

Cf. Dante's famous verse:

> Euclide geometra, e Tolomeo,
> Ippocrate, Avicenna e Galieno:
> Averrois, che'l gran commento feo.
> (*Inf.* IV, 142–144.)

Averroës is quoted here from L. GAUTHIER, *Accord de la religion et de la philosophie,* traduit et annoté, Imprimérie orientale Fontana, Alger, 1905, pp. 18–20. The arabic text has been published and translated into German by M. J. MÜLLER, *Philosophie und Theologie von Averroës,* München, 1859. An English translation of the same work has been published in India by M. JAMIL-UR-REHMAN, *The Philosophy of Averroës,* Baroda, 1921. For a detailed study of the problem, see E. RENAN, *Averroës et l'Averroisme, Essai historique,* Calmann-Lévy, Paris, 1852, and several later editions. In the third edition (1866), see esp. pp. 162–172; and L. GAUTHIER, *La théorie d'Ibn Rochd (Averroës) sur les rapports de la religion et de la philosophie,* E. Leroux, Paris, 1903; esp. pp. 177–182.

(2) AVERROËS, *Accord de la religion* . . ., pp. 21–26.

(3) AVERROËS, *Accord de la religion* . . ., p. 26.

(4) E. RENAN, *Averroës et l'Averroisme,* pp. 162–172, and the criticism (itself criticizable, but suggestive) of Renan's position, by L. GAUTHIER, *La théorie d'Ibn Rochd* . . ., pp. 1–18 and pp. 177–182.

(5) AVERROËS, *Accord de la religion* . . ., pp. 50–51.

(6) AVERROËS, *Accord de la religion* . . ., pp. 51–52. In the above-mentioned English translation, pp. 243–257.

The treatise of Averroës on the *Harmony of religion and philosophy* remained unknown to the Christian Theologians of the Middle Ages; but the last chapter of Averroës' *Destruction* contains a summary of his ideas on the question, and it was translated into Latin in the first third of the XIVth century. Cf. AVERROËS, *Destructio destructionum,* Disput. V, printed in the edition of Venice, apud Juntas, 1550, Vol. IX, f° 63.

(7) On the so-called doctrine of the twofold truth in Latin Averroism, see E. GILSON, *La doctrine de la double vérité,* in *Études de philosophie médiévale,* Strasbourg, 1921, pp. 50–69. In the very same year, and quite independently from the preceding article, an Italian scholar was reaching identically the same conclusion; cf. BRUNO NARDI, *Intorno alle dottrine filosofiche di Pietro d'Abano,* in Nuova Rivista Storica, Albrighi Segati, Milano, Vol. V, 2–3 (1921), pp. 34–35, and pp. 48–49.

(8) Dante has placed Siger of Brabant in his *Paradiso* (*Div. Comedy,* Parad., X, 133–138). The presence of a so well-known Averroist in Dante's heaven has given rise to endless controversies. The best explanation of that fact

seems to be that of Br. Nardi, viz. that Dante himself
being something of an Averroist, he could have no objec-
tions to Siger of Brabant (BR. NARDI, *Saggi de Filosofia
Dantesca,* Socanon Edit., Dante Alighieri, Milano, 1930).
There would be serious difficulty in admitting that conclusion, if the texts recently published by Fr. Van Steenberghen under the name of Siger could really be ascribed
to him; but the internal evidence is against it and the
external evidence is very weak, not to say non-existent.
Cf. Br. Nardi's article in *Giornale critico della filosofia
italiana,* 1936, pp. 26–35. An answer to Br. Nardi's criticism is announced by Fr. Van Steenberghen, in *Revue
Néoscolastique de Philosophie,* Vol. 40 (1937), pp 142–
144.

See G. DE LAGARDE, *La naissance de l'esprit laique au
déclin du moyen age,* Vol. II: *Marsile de Padoue ou le
premier théoricien de l'ésprit laique,* Editions Béatrice,
Saint-Paul-Trois-Chateaux, 1934.

(9) Those texts of John of Jaudun, together with
several other ones, have been collected in E. GILSON,
*Études de philosophie médiévale,* Strasbourg, 1921; pp.
70–75.

(10) On the continuity of the Averroistic tradition, see:
E. RENAN, *Averroës et l'Averroisme;* Paris, 1852. R.
CHARBONNEL, *La pensée italienne au XVIᵉ siecle et le
courant libertin;* Paris, Picard, 1904. H. BUSSON, *Les
sources et le développement du rationalisme dans la
littérature française de la Renaissance* (1533–1601).
Paris, Letouzey et Ané, 1922.

## CHAPTER III

(1) The Gnostic distinction between Faith, considered
as an inferior type of religious knowledge, and the
Gnosis, considered as an intellectual experience of religious truth, has never been accepted by any Father of the
Church or medieval theologian; to them, there was but
one Catholic faith, the same for all Christians, and one to

which the assent of the most learned theologians was just
as strictly bound as that of the most illiterate people.
Yet, Clement of Alexandria, for instance, certainly admitted of a hierarchy, if not of beliefs, at least of believers. His "Christian Gnostic" believes the same things
as all the other Christians, but his own faith is crowned
by a religious "knowledge" which is refused to common
believers (see the texts collected in G. Bardy, *Clément
d'Alexandrie*, J. Gabalda, Paris, 1926; pp. 246–312). A
slight touch of that aristocratic religious feeling can still
be detected in an early text of Saint Augustine: "nam
et a *melioribus* etiam dum has terras incolunt, et certe a
bonis et piis omnibus post hanc vitam . . ." (*De libero
arbitrio*, II, 2, 6). All good and pious men (*omnes*) will
see God in future life, but the *meliores* can already *know*
something about Him.

(2) THOMAS AQUINAS, *Summa Theologica*, Pt. II$^a$–
II$^{ae}$, qu. I, art. 5; transl. by the Fathers of the English
Dominican Province, pp. 10–13.

(3) THOMAS AQUINAS, *Summa contra Gentiles*, Bk.
II, Ch. 38; same transl. p. 83. Cf. Bk. I, Ch. 8; p. 15.

(4) THOMAS AQUINAS, *Summa Theologica*, Pt. I, qu.
46, art. 2, Answer; same transl., p. 250.

(5) THOMAS AQUINAS, *Summa Theologica*, Pt. II$^a$–
II$^{ae}$, qu. II, art. 4; pp. 36–37. *Summa contra Gentiles*,
Bk. I, Ch. 4; pp. 7–9.

(6) THOMAS AQUINAS, *Summa Theologica*, Pt. II$^a$–
II$^{ae}$, qu. I, art. 5, ad 3$^m$; p. 12. A complete exposition of
Saint Thomas' position will be found in: *In Boetium de
Trinitate*, qu. II, art. 3, Resp.; in *Opuscula omnia*, ed. P.
Mandonnet, Vol. III, p. 51.

(7) As translated by ALB. HYMA, *The Imitation of
Christ*, The Century Co., New York, 1927. In that edi-
tion, the second of the quoted texts will be found in Bk.
III, Ch. 35, p. 139.

(8) P. POURRAT, *Christian Spirituality in the Middle
Ages*, Burns Oates, London, 1924; Vol. II, pp. 253–256.

Cf. ALB. HYMA, *The Christian Renaissance: a History of the Devotio Moderna,* The Century Co., New York, 1925, and the Preface to the above-mentioned translation of *The Imitation of Christ,* pp. VII–XXXI.

(9) P. POURRAT, *op. cit.,* Vol. II, pp. 268–284.

(10) On that treatise, see M. WINDSTOSSER, *Étude sur la théologie germanique,* Paris, 1911.

(11) As translated in P. POURRAT, *op. cit.,* Vol. III, p. 78.

(12) See the remarkable essay of P. VIGNAUX, *Luther commentateur des sentences,* Paris, J. Vrin, 1935.

(13) M. LUTHER, *Disputatio contra scholasticam theologiam* (1517); Weimar edit., Vol. I, pp. 221–228. Cf. E. GILSON, *Le moyen âge et le naturalisme antique,* in *Archives d'histoire doctrinale et littéraire du moyen âge,* Vol. VII (1932), pp. 14–21.

(14) On the exact meaning of James' attitude towards the religious problem, see R. B. PERRY, *The Thought and Character of W. James;* Little, Brown and Co., Boston, 1935; Vol. I, pp. 164–166.

(15) H. BERGSON, *Les deux sources de la morale et de la religion,* Paris, F. Alcan, 1932; p. 256.

(16) R. OTTO, *The Idea of the Holy,* transl. by J. W. Harvey, Oxford Univ. Press, 4th edit., 1926, p. 182.

# INDEX
# OF NAMES

# Index of Names

Abelard, 12

Albertus Magnus (Saint Albert the Great), 14–15, 60, 70

Alexander of Hales, 70

Anselm, Saint, 22–27, 31, 32, 75, 81, 87

Aristotle, 6, 9, 12, 17, 38–39, 53, 79, 80, 93–94

Augustine, Saint, 16–24, 32

Averroes, 38–55, 58, 60, 64–66, 79–80, 84, 87

Avicenna, 38–39

Bacon, Francis, 95

Bacon, Roger, 28–30

Bergson, 96–98

Bernard, Saint, 12–13

Boethius of Dacia, 59, 65

Bonaventura, Saint, 22, 70

Cajetan, 84–85

Cano, M., 95

Clement of Alexandria, 16

Damiani, Saint Peter, 13

Dante, 60

Descartes, R., 95

Duns Scotus, 85–87, 90

Eckhart, Meister, 90

Epicureans, the, 6, 12, 17

Erasmus, Desiderius, 91–92, 94

Fontenelle, 65

Galileo, 37

Gaunilo, 25

Gazali, 39

Gerson, John, 90–91

Gioberti, 22

Groote, Gerhard (Groot, Gerritt), 90

Huesden, John Vos de, 91

James, William, 96–97

John of Jaudun, 61–63

John of Saint Thomas, 84

John, Saint, 16, 23

Justin Martyr, 16

Lull, Ramon, 30–31

Luther, Martin, 92–94

Maimonides, Moses, 69

Malebranche, 22, 32

Maritain, Jacques, 84

113